When I think of Tom I think about a night
When the earth smelled of summer
And the sky was streaked with white . . .
from THE KING AND I

Getting to Know You!

Rodgers and Hammerstein Favorites

Words by **Oscar Hammerstein II**

Music by **Richard Rodgers**

Illustrations by **Rosemary Wells**

HarperCollins*Publishers*

Contained within these pages are wonderful verses, originally set to equally wonderful music. Our fathers, Richard Rodgers and Oscar Hammerstein II, wrote the songs to eleven musicals. Theirs was such a seamless partnership that it is hard to read the words without hearing the music. Rodgers and Hammerstein shared an artistic vision and also a philosophy: They were devoted to celebrating good things, positive ideas, and good-hearted people.

Now, with this book, new generations of children will have the opportunity to experience sixteen of the timeless songs of our fathers, deliciously enhanced by Rosemary Wells's illustrations. These songs speak most to the experience of childhood—the wonder and delight of discovery and exploration. We envy the children—including our own grandchildren—for all the fun they are going to have.

—MARY RODGERS & WILLIAM HAMMERSTEIN

I was born in 1943, the year *Oklahoma!* opened. I remember certain things from that time: my mother's unlined face, my father's voice, and the radio singing the first songs I ever knew. They were "Oh, What a Beautiful Mornin'" and "The Surrey with the Fringe on Top." I sang them before I knew what the words meant.

Times have changed. Children no longer know these haunting melodies and lyrics as we once did. I would like the children who come after to me to know them.

—ROSEMARY WELLS

Younger than springtime are you,
Softer than starlight are you;
Gayer than laughter are you,
Sweeter than music are you . . .

Contents

Oh, What a Beautiful Mornin'

Getting to Know You

When the Children Are Asleep

All the sounds of the earth are like music.
All the sounds of the earth are like music.

There's a bright, golden haze on the meadow,

There's a bright, golden haze
on the meadow.

The corn is as high
as an elephant's eye,
An' it looks like it's climbin'
clear up to the sky.

Oh, what a beautiful mornin'!
Oh, what a beautiful day!
I got a beautiful feelin'
Ev'rythin's goin' my way.

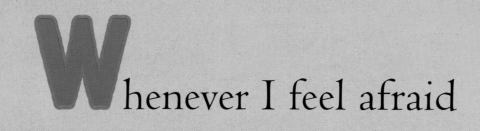

Whenever I feel afraid

I hold my head erect
And whistle a happy tune,
So no one will suspect I'm afraid.

 The result of this deception
Is very strange to tell,
For when I fool
the people I fear
I fool myself as well!

I whistle a happy tune,
And every single time
The happiness in the tune
Convinces me that I'm not afraid!

Make believe you're brave
And the trick will take you far;
You may be as brave
As you make believe you are.

The farmer and the cowman should be friends,

Oh, the farmer and the cowman
should be friends.

One man likes to push a plough,
the other likes to chase a cow,

But that's no reason why they can't be friends.

The farmer and the cowman should be friends,
Oh, the farmer and the cowman
should be friends.

The cowman ropes a cow with ease,
the farmer steals her butter and cheese,

But that's no reason why they can't be friends.

Cowboys dance with the farmers' daughters,

Farmers dance with the ranchers' gals.

19

appy talk,
Keep talkin' happy talk,
Talk about things you'd like to do.
You gotta have a dream;
If you don't have a dream,

CAFÉ
de la Palme

How you gonna have a dream come true?

Talk about a moon  Floatin' in the sky,

Lookin' like a lily on a lake;

Talk about a bird Learnin' how to fly,

Makin' all the music he can make—

Happy talk,
Keep talkin' happy talk,
Talk about things you'd like to do.
You gotta have a dream;
If you don't have a dream,
How you gonna have a dream come true?

Getting to know you,
Getting to know all about you,

Getting to like you,
Getting to hope you like me.

Getting to know you—
Putting it my way, but nicely,
You are precisely
My cup of tea!

Getting to know you, Getting to feel free and easy;

When I am with you, Getting to know what to say—

Haven't you noticed? Suddenly I'm bright and breezy

Because of All the beautiful and new Things I'm learning about you,

Day by day.

I'm gonna wash that man right outa my hair,
I'm gonna wash that man right outa my hair,

I'm gonna wash that man right outa my hair
And send him on his way.

Dites-moi Pourquoi
La vie est belle,

Dites-moi
Pourquoi
La vie est gai?

Dites-moi Pourquoi,
Chère mad'moiselle,
Est-ce que Parce que vous m'aimez?

Chicks and ducks and geese better scurry

When I take you out in the surrey,
When I take you out in the surrey
with the fringe on top.

Watch that fringe and see how it flutters
When I drive them high-steppin' strutters—
Nosey-pokes'll peek through their shutters
and their eyes will pop!

The wind'll whistle as we rattle along,

The cows'll moo in the clover,

The river will ripple out a whispered song,

And whisper it over and over:

Don't you wisht you'd go on ferever and would never stop

In that shiny little surrey with the fringe on the top?

His name is Mister Snow

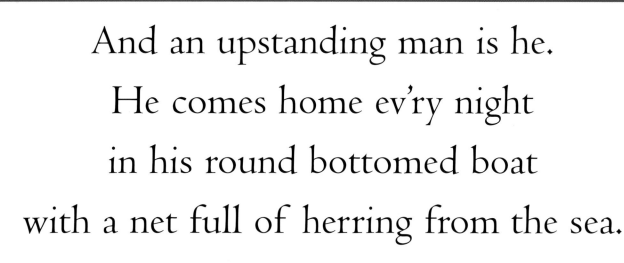

And an upstanding man is he.

He comes home ev'ry night

in his round bottomed boat

with a net full of herring from the sea.

An almost perfect beau,

As refined as a girl could wish,

But he spends so much time
in his round bottomed boat,
That he can't seem to lose the smell of fish!
The first time he kissed me,

The whiff of his clothes
knocked me flat on the floor of the room.

But now that I love him,
my heart's in my nose

And fish is my fav'rit perfume.

When I marry Mister Snow,
The flowers'll be buzzin' with the hum of bees,

The birds'll make a racket in the churchyard trees,
When I marry Mister Snow.

OKLAHOMA

Where the wind comes
sweepin' down the plain,

And the wavin' wheat ★ Can sure smell sweet
When the wind comes right behind the rain.

OKLAHOMA!

Every night my honey lamb and I

Sit alone and talk ★ And watch a hawk

Makin' lazy circles in the sky.

We know we belong to the land,
And the land we belong to is grand.

And when we say:

Ee-ee-ow!   A-yip-i-o-ee-ay!

We're only sayin', ⭐ You're doin' fine, Oklahoma!

OKLAHOMA, O.K.!

When the Children Are Asleep

W
hen the children are asleep,
we'll sit and dream
The things that ev'ry other
dad and mother dream.

When the children are asleep and lights are low,
If I still love you the way I love you today,
You'll pardon my saying "I told you so!"
When the children are asleep, I'll dream with you.

This was a real nice clambake, We're mighty glad we came.
The vittles we et Were good, you bet! The company was the same.

Our hearts are warm,  Our bellies are full, And we are feelin' prime.

This was a real nice clambake, And we all hed a real good time.

Shall we dance?

On a bright cloud of music shall we fly?

Shall we dance?

Shall we then say "good night"

and mean "good-bye"?

Or, perchance,

When the last little star

has left the sky,

Shall we still be together

With our arms around each other

And shall you be my new romance?

On the clear understanding

That this kind of thing can happen,

Shall we dance?

Shall we dance?

Shall we dance?

If I loved you,
Time and again I would try to say
All I'd want you to know.

If I loved you,
Words wouldn't come in an easy way—
Round in circles I'd go.

Longin' to tell you,
but afraid and shy,
I'd let my golden chances pass me by.
Soon you'd leave me,
Off you would go in the mist of day,

Never, never to know
How I loved you—
If I loved you.

Most people live on a lonely island,
Lost in the middle of a foggy sea.
Most people long for another island,
One where they know they would like to be.

Bali Ha'i 🍃 Will whisper
On the wind 🍃 Of the sea:
"Here am I, 🍃 Your special island!
Come to me, 🍃 Come to me!"
If you try, 🍃 You'll find me
Where the sky 🍃 Meets the sea;
"Here am I, 🍃 Your special island!
Come to me, 🍃 Come to me!"

S ome enchanted evening

Someone may be laughing,

You may hear her laughing

Across a crowded room—

And night after night,
As strange as it seems,
The sound of her laughter
will sing in your dreams.

Getting to Know You!: *Rodgers and Hammerstein Favorites*
Compilation copyright © 2002 by Williamson Music   Illustrations copyright © 2002 by Rosemary Wells
"Mr. Snow" illustration on page 37 copyright © 2001 by Rosemary Wells
Illustration originally appeared on the cover of the October 2001 issue of *Cricket* magazine.
Printed in Hong Kong. All rights reserved.   www.harperchildrens.com
Library of Congress Cataloging-in-Publication Data   Rodgers, Richard.   [Musicals. Librettos. Selections]
Getting to know you! Rodgers and Hammerstein favorites   words by Oscar Hammerstein II ;
music by Richard Rodgers ; illustrations by Rosemary Wells.   p. cm   ISBN 0-06-027925-7—
ISBN 0-06-623845-5 (lib. bdg.)   1. Musicals—Excerpts—Librettos   2. Popular music—Texts.
[1. Songs. 2. Popular music. 3. Musicals—Excerpts.]   I. Hammerstein, Oscar, 1895–1960.   II. Wells, Rosemary,
ill.   III. Title   ML49.R67 M86 2002   782.1'40268–dc21   2001016847
1 2 3 4 5 6 7 8 9 10
❖
First Edition